# The Shepherd And His Sheep

Eight Children's Sermons
And Activity Pages
For Lent And Easter

## Julia E. Bland

CSS Publishing Company, Inc., Lima, Ohio

THE SHEPHERD AND HIS SHEEP

*In memory of my mother,
Lillian Mary Johnson Bell*

Copyright © 2001 by
CSS Publishing Company, Inc.
Lima, Ohio

The original purchaser may photocopy material in this publication for use as it was intended (i.e. worship material for worship use; educational material for classroom use; dramatic material for staging or production). No additional permission is required from the publisher for such copying by the original purchaser only. Inquiries should be addressed to: Permissions, CSS Publishing Company, Inc., P.O. Box 4503, Lima, Ohio 45802-4503.

Scripture quotations are from the *New Revised Standard Version of the Bible*, copyright 1989 by the Division of Christian Education of the National Council of the Churches of Christ in the USA. Used by permission.

ISBN: 0-7880-1860-4              PRINTED IN U.S.A.

# Table Of Contents

| | |
|---|---:|
| Introduction And Suggestions From The Author | 4 |
| Children's Sermons | |
|     Lent 1: The Shepherd And His Sheep<br>        John 10:14, 26-27 | 5 |
|     Lent 2: The Shepherd Knows<br>        John 10:3b, 14, 27 | 6 |
|     Lent 3: The Sheep Hear And Follow<br>        John 10:4-5, 27 | 7 |
|     Lent 4: Jesus Is The Gate<br>        John 10:9 | 8 |
|     Lent 5: Other Sheep, One Flock<br>        John 10:16 | 9 |
|     Lent 6/Passion Sunday: Willing To Die<br>        John 10:11-13, 15, 18; See also Luke 15:3-7 | 10 |
|     Easter Sunday: The Shepherd Is Alive!<br>        John 10:17b-18, 10, 28; Psalm 23 | 11 |
|     Sunday Following Easter: Shepherd's Helpers<br>        John 21:15; 1 Peter 5:4 | 13 |
| Children's Activity Pages | 15 |
| Answer Keys | 31 |
| Easter Story Folder | 35 |

# Introduction And Suggestions From The Author

The land of Judea was better suited for pasture than agriculture. Raising sheep was, therefore, of great importance. The theme of shepherd and sheep runs through both the Old and the New Testaments. The hard life of the shepherds was truly one of self-sacrifice. Constant watching, unfailing courage, patience, and love for the flock were the characteristics of the shepherd. This is a perfect picture of Jesus, our Good Shepherd.

These lessons are based on Jesus' statement in John 10 that he is the Good Shepherd. We hope to learn a little of what he meant.

The lessons are planned so that each child may take back to the pew an activity sheet. One side is a coloring page for young children. The other side has word puzzles and games for older children. The lessons are not limited to morning worship, however. They may be used any time there is opportunity for Christian education of children.

Study the sermon so that you can tell it in your own words, using your own personality and with the needs of your children in mind.

The sermon as given is to get you started. Be open to the Holy Spirit as he guides you to add your own personal observations.

If you need notes, make them small and tuck them inside your Bible at the page where you will be reading the Scripture.

Open the Bible and read from it. Children need to know that what you say really is from the Scriptures.

Ask questions and allow time for the children to answer. This will get them thinking and involved, but children can say unexpected things, so be ready to guide them back to the subject.

Before the worship hour, clip the activity sheet, a pencil, and crayons to a clipboard to be ready to hand to each child when the children's time is over.

As you pray and prepare, claim the Lord's promise in Isaiah 55:11:

*So shall my word be that goes out from my mouth;*
*it shall not return to me empty,*
*but it shall accomplish that which I purpose,*
*and succeed in the thing for which I sent it.*

God will help and bless your efforts.

Julia E. Bland

# Lent 1: The Shepherd And His Sheep

*Jesus is the Good Shepherd of those who listen and follow him.*

**Scripture:** John 10:14, 26-27

**Background Devotions:** John 10:1-30

**Visual Aids:** Something made of wool

**Handouts:** Activity sheets

**Advance Preparations:** Copy enough activity pages for each child to have one.

**The Lesson:**

I have something here that is made of wool.* *(Show and explain)* Wool is very warm and will last a lifetime if I take care of it. Do you know where wool comes from? Wool comes from sheep. When a sheep's coat gets long and full in late spring, it is cut, spun into yarn, and then woven into cloth. People have been using wool from sheep for hundreds of years, even before Jesus lived. Sheep were raised for other purposes too, but wool for clothing was one of the main reasons.

Sheep were very valuable at the time when Jesus lived. Do you have a pet? A cat or a dog? Families back then had a lamb, a baby sheep, for a pet. It would come in the house and sleep with its family just like our dog or cat might do.

Sheep are kind of helpless and have to have lots of care, and there were special people who took care of them. Do you know what they were called? Yes, shepherds. A good shepherd was a very special kind of person, for he loved his sheep very much and would do anything necessary to take good care of them. The sheep knew this and they loved their shepherd, too. Sheep that were kept for wool lived many years with their own shepherd.

When Jesus taught, he used things that everyone knew about to help people to understand him better. Everyone where Jesus lived knew about sheep and shepherds because raising sheep was such an important business at that time and place. So one day Jesus said, "I am the good shepherd, I know my own and my own know me" (John 10:14).

For a few Sundays we are thinking of how much Jesus loved us, enough to die for us. Let's see if we can understand some of the things he meant when he said he was the good shepherd.

If Jesus is the good shepherd who loves and cares for his sheep, who do you think he meant that the sheep are? Jesus tells us in John 10:27, "My sheep hear my voice. I know them and they follow me."

So is everyone a sheep in Jesus' flock? No. We wish everyone was, but only those who hear and follow Jesus are. Jesus said in John 10:26, "You do not believe ... you do not belong to my sheep."

He was talking to some folks there who did not believe what he was saying. So who are the sheep? Jesus said it was those who believe in him, those who hear him, and those who follow him.

To believe in Jesus means believing he is truly the Son of God, that he came to earth, died for us, and was raised to life again. To follow Jesus means that we try hard to do what he says and live life like he wants us to. It means to love him most of all.

Jesus is the good shepherd who loves and takes care of those who believe in him and do what he asks. We will be talking about Jesus the Good Shepherd again.

*Use visual aids

# Lent 2: The Shepherd Knows
*Jesus the Good Shepherd loves us, knows our name and all about us.*

**Scripture:** John 10:3b, 14, 27

**Background Devotions:** Psalm 100:3; 95:6-7

**Visual Aids:** A name tag

**Handouts:** Activity sheets; a name tag for each child if desired

**Advance Preparations:** Copy enough activity pages for each child to have one.

**The Lesson:**

There is something that is all yours and very special to you. It is your name. When you were born, your mom and dad tried very hard to give you the best of names. Sometimes names have a special meaning. That was especially so with Bible names. For instance, Peter means "rock," David means "beloved," Sarah means "princess," and Anna means "Jehovah (God) has been gracious." We might name a baby Joy because she brought happiness when she was born, or Dawn because she was born early in the morning. We might name a baby Sam, because that was Grandpa's name and we loved Grandpa so much.

Once in a while someone will have the same name as we do. That can be confusing. But we can usually figure a way to avoid mix-ups by using initials or middle names, too.

I have a name tag.* Name tags are very helpful. People wear them in a crowd. It helps us get acquainted and remember who everyone is. Sometimes it is very hard to remember everyone's name. A name tag helps.

But Jesus does not need us to wear a name tag.* Jesus knows who every one of us are and he knows all our names. John 10:3b says, "He [the shepherd] calls his own sheep by name and leads them out."

During this time of Lent, the days before Easter, we are talking about Jesus as the Good Shepherd. Jesus called himself the good shepherd. If Jesus is the shepherd, who are the sheep? John 10:27 says that those who listen to Jesus and follow him are his sheep. That means those who believe in him and try hard to do what he says.

When Jesus lived and taught, keeping sheep was something everyone knew about because keeping sheep was an important business at that time and place. So when Jesus said he was the good shepherd, everyone could understand what he meant. They all knew how a good shepherd loved and cared for his sheep. Most sheep were kept for their wool and so they lived many years with their shepherd.

A good shepherd knew all his sheep very well and could call them by name, like Black Ear, Sweet Pea, Black Sox, or Black Tail. All had names and the shepherd knew each one. The shepherd knew all about his sheep. He knew if Black Ear was lazy, Sweet Pea was nervous, Black Sox was bad-tempered, or Black Tail liked to wander away. The shepherd knew all this about his sheep and loved and took care of all.

Jesus is like the shepherd. He said in John 10:14, "I am the good shepherd, I know my own and my own know me." So he knows all about us and takes care of us, his sheep. Doesn't it make you feel happy and good to know that Jesus knows your name and all about you and loves you just the way you are and wants to help and take care of you? Jesus knows and loves each of us.

*Use visual aids

# Lent 3: The Sheep Hear And Follow
*Jesus our Good Shepherd wants us to spend time with him.*

**Scripture:** John 10:4-5, 27

**Background Devotions:** Isaiah 40:10-11

**Visual Aids:** A Bible

**Handouts:** Activity sheets

**Advance Preparations:** Copy enough activity pages for each child to have one.

**The Lesson:**

When Jesus lived, there were many flocks of sheep. Sheep were important at that time. They were used in worship, for food and milk, and kept for their wool. Shepherds took care of sheep. They lived with their flock and knew each of their sheep by name. In cold weather, sheep spent nights close to town in a place made for them. There would be many flocks kept in the same place but each with its own shepherd. In the morning the shepherd would come to the gate and call his sheep. The sheep recognized the voice of their shepherd and followed him out of the gate and up into the hills. No sheep would ever follow unless it recognized its own shepherd's voice. Instead it would wait until it heard the voice it knew. Jesus said in John 10:4-5:

> *"When he [the shepherd] has brought out all his own, he goes ahead of them, and the sheep follow him because they know his voice. They will not follow a stranger, but they will run from him because they do not know the voice of strangers."*

It was different in warm weather. The sheep stayed out on the hillside all the time, night and day, and their shepherd stayed with them. Then sometimes different shepherds would visit together on the hillside and sheep of different flocks got mixed together. But no one ever worried; all the shepherd had to do was call his own sheep and they would follow, leaving the other flocks behind. Sheep always followed their own shepherd, never a stranger.

Jesus said *he* was the good shepherd and we are his sheep if we hear and follow him (John 10:27). How do we hear our shepherd's voice so that we can follow him? He speaks to us today through the Bible.* Many years ago people who heard him teach wrote his words down and we have them here.* That is why the Bible is so special. It has the words of Jesus our shepherd. We listen to his words from the Bible* and like good sheep we follow and try to do and live just like he says.

When the shepherd called his sheep, they followed. He went ahead of them to make sure the way was safe. He led them to places where they could safely eat and drink.

During the day each sheep spent some time with the shepherd. Each one would take its turn coming to the shepherd to rub against him, or if the shepherd was sitting, the sheep would rub its cheek against his face or nibble at his ear. Then the shepherd spoke to his sheep and scratched its nose and ears, petting each of his sheep in this loving way.

Jesus is our shepherd. We should be like those sheep. We, too, should spend some time with our shepherd. We do this by prayer, by reading his words in the Bible, or by just thinking about Jesus with love. We can also come to him in worship when we gather with our church. This is very important. Every day we need to spend some time some way with our shepherd.

*Use visual aids

# Lent 4: Jesus Is The Gate
*It is through Jesus, the Good Shepherd, that we become part of his flock.*

**Scripture:** John 10:9

**Background Devotions:** Psalm 23

**Visual Aids:** Medicine, a large cup, perhaps a cane. If a cane is used, you will need to explain that the staff was shaped something like a cane but it was much longer and the rounded part was bigger.

**Handouts:** Activity sheets; star stickers for the color page of the activity sheet, if desired

**Advance Preparations:** Copy enough activity pages for each child to have one.

**The Lesson:**

When Jesus lived there were lots of sheep. Everyone knew about sheep and shepherds and how shepherds loved their sheep very much and would do everything possible to take good care of them. So when Jesus said he was the good shepherd, he hoped everyone who heard him would understand how, like a shepherd, he loves us and wants to take care of us.

If Jesus is like a good shepherd, why are we like sheep? Maybe it is because sheep are helpless and need lots of care. We do too.

When the weather was warm, the flocks stayed out on the hillsides day and night. The shepherd was with them, too, day and night. All day long he watched and cared for his sheep. He made sure there was plenty to eat and drink. Sheep are afraid of running water so sometimes the shepherd had to make a little dam to collect water into a quiet pool. He had to watch so that there were no poisonous plants to make his sheep sick. Sometimes the shepherd had to lead his sheep on a scary path to get to a place for feeding on better grass. If a sheep should fall or stumble, the shepherd could catch it by the rounded end of his staff.\* The staff circled the sheep around its neck or chest and the sheep was pulled back to safety.

In the evening when it was time for bed, the shepherd led his sheep to a walled-in place. This place was made of stones had no roof. It had an opening but no door or gate to open and close. As each sheep entered through the opening, the shepherd stopped it.

He looked to see if his sheep had any stickers caught in its coat or any scratches, snake bites, or hurts of any kind. If so, he carefully cleaned and put medicine\* on the hurting places. Then the shepherd gave each sheep a drink from a cup\* he had dipped into a big jug of water.

When all the sheep were in, the shepherd wrapped himself in his woolen robe and lay down across the opening facing the sheep. He became the gate and the sheep slept safely with the shepherd guarding the doorway. Nothing and no one could get to the sheep because the shepherd was there in the gateway keeping them safe.

The people Jesus taught knew how a shepherd guarded his sheep at the opening all through the night. So Jesus said in John 10:9: "I am the gate. Whoever enters by me will be saved, and will come in and go out and find pasture."

Jesus wanted them and us to understand that only through Jesus can anyone enter and become part of his flock. This verse says they can come in and go out. That means *we* can come and go secure in God's love and care. The pasture we find means that Jesus' sheep will have all the care we need and life will be good.

Aren't you glad Jesus said he was our shepherd?

\*Use visual aids

# Lent 5: Other Sheep, One Flock
*Jesus, our Good Shepherd, brings us together with all kinds of people.*

**Scripture:** John 10:16

**Background Devotions:** Ezekiel 34:11-16

**Visual Aids:** A globe or map

**Handouts:** Activity sheets

**Advance Preparations:** Copy enough activity pages for each child to have one.

**The Lesson:**

We are talking about Jesus the Good Shepherd again today. When Jesus said he was the good shepherd, what did he mean? He cares for his people like a shepherd cares for sheep. Good shepherds think there is nothing as important as their sheep. When Jesus lived, shepherds went out to live with their sheep, spending day and night with them. That's why they knew each other so well. Doesn't that sound like Jesus? He came to live on earth with us like a shepherd does and that is why we have learned so much about him and our Heavenly Father and God's love for us.

Jesus is the shepherd. Who are the sheep? We have learned that those who believe and listen and follow Jesus are his sheep. Not everyone does. We wish everyone did. If you love Jesus, believe and try to do as he said, you are one of his sheep. Or maybe we should say one of his little lambs, since you are not grown up yet.

Some of the people Jesus was talking to when he said that he was the good shepherd did not believe him. They did not believe he was God's Son. Some of them thought they already knew everything there was to know. Some of them thought that they were the only ones who did know. They even thought they were the only ones God cared about. No one, besides themselves, was important or loved by God, they thought. Some people today act like that, too. They act like they think their town, their school, or their church is all that is important to God and even that God loves them better than anyone else. Jesus had something to say about this in John 10:16: "I have other sheep that do not belong to this fold. I must bring them also and they will listen to my voice. So there will be one flock, one shepherd."

Jesus said there are others! Do you see this globe* (map)? Let's find about where we live. It is a very small place when we look at all the other places where people live, too. Two thousand years have passed since Jesus taught that there were others. Since then all kinds of people all around the world* have believed and followed Jesus — people from all nations, languages, colors, poor, rich, other churches, and maybe even some folks we don't like much. All will be part of Jesus' one flock if they believe in him, listen to what he says, and try to do it.

Loving Jesus is the way that all people are brought together. If Jesus accepts all who believe, we need to accept them, too. Together we can say Jesus is *our* shepherd, God is *our* Father, and we are brothers and sisters. When we can all live together like this, in love, good things are bound to happen!

*Use visual aids

# Lent 6/Passion Sunday: Willing To Die
*Jesus, our Good Shepherd, died for us, his sheep.*

**Scripture:** John 10:11-13, 15, 18; see also Luke 15:3-7

**Background Devotions:** Isaiah 53

**Visual Aids:** A cross. A small cross can be made using two rough twigs or branches. Glue or tie them together. An ugly cross gets the point across. If you'd like, make one for each child.

**Handouts:** Activity sheets; small crosses, if desired

**Advance Preparations:** Copy enough activity pages for each child to have one.

**The Lesson:**

Jesus is our shepherd. He cares for us like a good shepherd will care for his sheep. It was easy for a sheep to get lost in the days when Jesus was teaching. There were no fences and a sheep might put its nose down and go from one juicy plant to another, never bothering to look up to see where the shepherd or the rest of the flock was. A good shepherd would go looking for the lost sheep, looking and looking until he found it. He would then lay it across his shoulder and bring it back, happy and rejoicing because he'd found his sheep. Jesus said (Luke 15:3-7) that when this happened the shepherd called together his friends and they all celebrated because they were so happy that the lost one had been found. Jesus said that in heaven there is rejoicing, too, each time someone trusts Jesus as their savior and becomes part of his flock.

Jesus said something else in John 10:12. He said that a person who is not the good shepherd, who only works taking care of the sheep to get paid, does not own the sheep and does not really love them. So if wild animals, such as wolves, come trying to kill a sheep that person will run away and leave the sheep for the wolves. But Jesus said the real shepherd loves his sheep and will stay and fight the wolves away even if he must give his life and die to protect them. Jesus said he is like that. Jesus said he was going to die to save his sheep. John 10:11, "I am the good shepherd. The good shepherd lays down his life for the sheep." In verse 15b he said it again, "I lay down my life for the sheep." Then Jesus said in John 10:18, "No one takes it [his life] from me but I lay it down of my own accord."

We might think that those people killed Jesus and he couldn't get away from them, but that is not true. Jesus willingly let them put him on the cross.* The cross was an ugly thing. Jesus knew it would be a terrible way to die, yet he was willing to do it because he loves us so much. All of us think or do wrong things sometimes. That makes us sinners. Jesus' death on the cross brings forgiveness to us from God. We don't have to pay for our sins because Jesus did. Our Good Shepherd took care of us.

So today and for the coming week, God's people, his sheep, will be thinking about Jesus, our wonderful shepherd, and how he gave his life for us.

Isn't Jesus a wonderful Good Shepherd?

*Use visual aids

# Easter 7: The Shepherd Is Alive!
*Jesus, our Good Shepherd, is alive!*

**Scripture:** John 10:17b-18, 10, 28; Psalm 23

**Background Devotions:** Hebrews 13:20-21

**Visual Aids:** The story folder

**Handouts:** Activity sheets and story folder

**Advance Preparations:** Copy enough activity pages for each child to have one. Fold the story the long way, then the short way, so that the pages will be in order from 1 to 4. Be ready to give each child the folder when you begin the lesson.

**The Lesson:**

I have a story folder for you. It will help us remember the things we have been learning about sheep and shepherds and Jesus our Good Shepherd. Let's see what it says.

Page 1. Sheep hear and follow their shepherd.
He knows them all by name.
Jesus is the Good Shepherd.

Jesus said all who believe in him, listen to him, and follow him are his sheep. He knows every one of us, our names and all about us.

Page 2. Sheep and shepherd spend time together.
The shepherd is the gate to the flock.

Jesus wants us, his sheep, to listen to what he says in the Bible and spend time with him in prayer. Jesus said he was the gate and all who are part of his flock must enter through him. That means we are his sheep in his flock, if we believe in Jesus and love him.

Page 3. The shepherd has other sheep.
He is willing to die for them all.
Jesus died for us.

Jesus said there would be many others who would also be part of his flock. Jesus said a good shepherd would give his life to save his sheep, and Jesus our Good Shepherd did give his life for us. We know now how much God loves us all.

But Jesus was not an ordinary shepherd. He said in John 10:17b-18: "I lay down my life in order to take it up again. No one takes it from me, but I lay it down of my own accord. I have power to lay it down, and I have power to take it up again." What does he mean when he says he will take up his life again? He means he will be raised back to life! And that is just what we celebrate today! Jesus didn't stay dead.

Page 4.  Jesus is alive!
He is still our shepherd!

And because he lives, he promised this life to us, too. We are his sheep. If we believe in him, listen to him and follow him, and try to do as he asks, we are his sheep and we will have life just as he does. That means life now and forever.

Jesus continues to be our shepherd, even though he has gone back to heaven. When he left, he sent his Holy Spirit to live with us, helping. Jesus continues to care for his people like a shepherd cares for his sheep. What does a shepherd do caring for his sheep? Psalm 23 gives us a little idea. It tells us that a shepherd leads his sheep to food and water and rest. He leads his sheep along paths that are good. When the path is dark and scary or hard, he protects his sheep. He protects them from enemies with his rod and staff and anoints each sheep with oil for healing. All of this means a good, happy life for the sheep.

We are not real sheep. We work hard for things we need, but Jesus, our Good Shepherd, promises to help and give us a good and happy life with things that money cannot buy, things like love, joy, peace, and eternal life with him.

In John 10:10, Jesus calls this abundant life — life that is more than enough. Of course, these good things in life do not come unless we are willing to listen and follow Jesus. In John 10:28, Jesus tells us that this life Jesus gives never ends. To die is the beginning of even better life. It tells us that the life Jesus gives is secure. No one can take his sheep from him. Even when bad things happen, the sheep know that their shepherd is with them to help.

Isn't Jesus a wonderful shepherd?


*Use visual aids

# 8. Sunday Following Easter: Shepherd's Helpers
*We are the Good Shepherd's helpers.*

**Scripture:** John 21:15; 1 Peter 5:4

**Background Devotions:** John 21:1-19; 1 Peter 5:1-4; Acts 20:28

**Visual Aids:** A fork, a spoon, crackers, an apple, a Bible

**Handouts:** Activity sheets; snacks, if desired

**Advance Preparations:** Copy enough activity pages for each child to have one.

**The Lesson:**
Have you ever been hungry? There's an empty place in your stomach, isn't there? It doesn't feel good to have an empty stomach. Sometimes it makes us feel grouchy, unhappy, or maybe even weak.

What should we do? Yes, eat something. Maybe it is dinner time* and we'll have meat, potatoes, vegetables, and fruit. If it is lunch time, we might have a sandwich or soup.* But if it is not really time to eat, a little snack such as crackers* or an apple* will do. Then in a few minutes we feel much better.

There is another way to feel empty. It can make us unhappy, too. It can make us grouchy and weak. There is an unhappy empty place inside us when we do not make Jesus our Lord and let him be part of our lives. We need Jesus to fill us up with happiness and the help we need to live good lives.

Last Sunday we talked about Jesus, our Good Shepherd, and how he rose from the dead. It was Easter and we celebrated. He is still alive! Before Jesus went back to heaven to be with his Heavenly Father, he spent some time with his friends. There were still some things he wanted to tell them. One day he had breakfast with them. John 21:15 says:

> *When they had finished breakfast, Jesus said to Simon Peter, "Simon, son of John, do you love me more than these?" He said to him, "Yes, Lord; you know that I love you." Jesus said to him, "Feed my lambs."*

Jesus said, "Peter, I want you to feed my lambs and tend my sheep." When Jesus asked Peter to feed his lambs, he was talking about his people; he called those who loved him his sheep. Now Peter is asked to feed them. Jesus does not mean meat and potatoes. He means that Peter is to teach and preach about Jesus and his love, to fill up the empty, unhappy, hungry places in the lives of those who need to know about Jesus. Peter did as Jesus asked.

Today we still have people who do as Jesus asked Peter to do. They are called pastors. The word *pastor* comes from the word *pasture*. Our churches, the congregations, are sometimes called flocks. Our pastors are to feed their flocks, giving God's Word,* helping people fill up the empty places in the lives of all who need to know more about Jesus. They are shepherds helping Jesus do the work of caring for Jesus' sheep until the day when Jesus, who is the Chief Shepherd, comes back again (1 Peter 5:4).

This is a big job. We can help. We can all be shepherds' helpers when we share Jesus and his love with others, when we love and help and share. Let's all be shepherds' helpers. This will please Jesus, our Good Shepherd.

*Use visual aids

**Lent 1**

**Sheep hear and follow their Good Shepherd.**

**The words that are underlined are in the word search puzzle. They will go down or left to right.**

| S | H | E | E | P | M | E | A | N | S | D | O |
|---|---|---|---|---|---|---|---|---|---|---|---|
| L | U | Y | E | A | R | S | O | J | X | T | P |
| I | S | G | O | O | D | H | F | E | B | R | E |
| F | H | U | N | D | R | E | D | S | E | Y | O |
| E | E | H | C | T | O | W | O | U | L | D | P |
| O | P | I | A | I | N | P | X | S | I | I | L |
| W | H | M | R | H | E | A | R | S | E | E | E |
| N | E | C | E | S | S | A | R | Y | V | D | W |
| W | R | C | A | M | E | S | O | N | E | H | O |
| A | D | R | A | I | S | E | D | X | S | E | O |
| S | S | A | Y | S | F | O | L | L | O | W | L |
| E | V | E | R | Y | O | N | E | A | R | T | H |

People have been using wool from sheep for hundreds of years. When Jesus lived, there were shepherds who took care of sheep. A good shepherd would do everything necessary to take good care of his sheep. Jesus said he was the good shepherd. Everyone who believes in him, hears him, and follows him are his sheep. To believe in Jesus means that we believe he is God's own son who came to earth, died for us, and was raised to life again. To follow Jesus means that we love him and we try hard to do what he says.

**Across**

_____ are animals that need lots of care.

**Down**

A _____ is someone who gives that care.

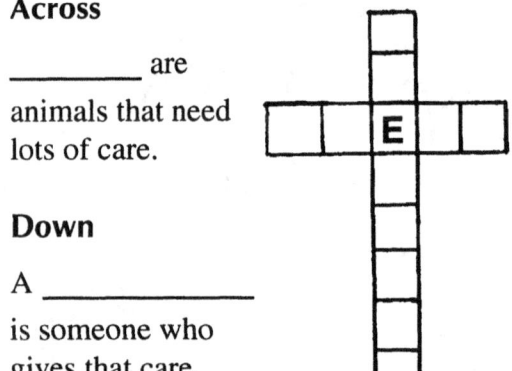

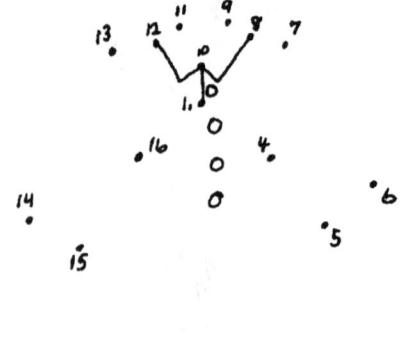

Sometimes a _ _ _ _ is made of wool.

**Can you unscramble these words? They are all found in the Bible verses below.**

ownk _ _ _ _  
mhte _ _ _ _  
icevo _ _ _ _ _  
odog _ _ _ _  
rhae _ _ _ _  

peesh _ _ _ _ _  
em _ _  
wno _ _ _  
ololwf _ _ _ _ _ _  
erdshpeh _ _ _ _ _ _ _ _  

**Jesus said this:**

"I am the good shepherd. I know my own and my own know me."
John 10:14

"My sheep hear my voice. I know them and they follow me."
John 10:27

**Did you know ...**

A shepherd dressed for comfort and convenience. He wore an undergarment called a tunic. Over this he wore a four-foot square wool cloak which shielded him from sun, rain, or snow. He could pull it over his head like a tent for shelter at night. It usually had big grey and black stripes and was woven by his wife or daughters. He folded a piece of cloth around his waist and kept small things in that. It was called a girdle. The shepherd had a veil for his head. It was about 36-inches square and was folded into a triangle and kept in place by a ring of twisted goat's hair. He had long hair and a beard because that was easiest to care for.

Lent 2

**The Good Shepherd knows each sheep by name.**

**The words that are underlined are in the word search puzzle. See if you can find them.**

There is <u>something</u> that is all ours and <u>very</u> <u>special</u> to us. It is our <u>name</u>. It is <u>sometimes</u> <u>hard</u> to <u>remember</u> everyone's name. But <u>Jesus</u> knows <u>all</u> of <u>our</u> names. He <u>knows</u> all <u>about</u> us, too, just like a <u>shepherd</u> knew the name of each <u>sheep</u> <u>in</u> his flock. He knew all about <u>each</u> <u>one</u> <u>too</u>, because shepherds who <u>kept</u> sheep for their <u>wool</u> <u>lived</u> with their sheep many <u>years</u>, taking <u>care</u> of them. Jesus is the <u>good</u> shepherd. He <u>loves</u> each one of <u>us</u>. <u>If</u> we <u>listen</u> to <u>him</u> and follow him, <u>we</u> are sheep of his <u>flock</u>.

```
V L O V E S F L O C K L
E A N K N O W S H S J I
R B E N A M E X I H E V
Y O S O M E T I M E S E
H U K S U T A L L P U D
A T E H S H E A C H S G
R S P E C I A L Y E W O
D O T E A N I F E R O O
T U X P R G W F A D O D
O R E M E M B E R X L I
O L I S T E N X S I N S
```

**Did you know ...**

Sheep were raised for many purposes. They provided food, meat, milk, and fat from the tail. Sheep horns could be made into a musical instrument or a flask, which is a bottle. Sheep were used as sacrifices in worship. They provided clothing; sometimes the whole skin was used, but more often the wool was cut, spun, and woven into clothing for all the family. Cutting sheep wool was done in late spring and was a time of celebration, for the wool was valuable. Friends were often invited to share a happy meal during this time of celebration.

Sometimes a _ _ _ _ _ _ _ is made of wool.

**Down**
Jesus, the good shepherd, _____ our name.

**Across**
Jesus knows all _____ us.

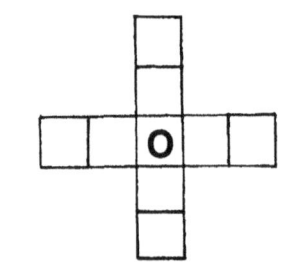

**Use the words below to finish the sentences.**

Sheep were _____.

They were kept for their _____.

Shepherds loved their _____.

They knew the names of _____.

Sheep come when the shepherd _____.

Our name is _____.

Name tags help us _____.

Jesus is the good _____.

He knows our _____.

He knows all about ___.

He loves us just like we _____.

We need to follow _____.

We will do as he _____.

are
says
shepherd
remember
special
valuable
wool
sheep
all
name
us
him
calls

**Lent 3**

**Sheep spend time with their Good Shepherd.**

**This sheep wants to spend time with the shepherd. Help it find the way.**

**Did you know ...**

If all the sheep were doing well and the shepherd had a little free time, he would sometimes make a musical pipe from reeds, which were a kind of grass with a hollow stem. Sometimes he used a ram's horn to play music. A ram is a male sheep.

The Bible tells us that before David became king of Israel, he was a shepherd. He played a lyre, sometimes called a harp. He played so well that he was asked to play for the king. This story is found in 1 Samuel 16:12-23.

Sometimes a

_ _ _ _ _ _ _

is made of wool.

**Jesus said this:**

I am the good shepherd. I know my own and my own know me. He [the shepherd] calls his own sheep by name and leads them out. When he has brought out all his own, he goes ahead of them and the sheep follow him because they know his voice.   (John 10:14, 3, 5)

**Can you unscramble these words? They are all found in the Bible verses above. When you are finished, find the same words in the word search puzzle. They will go left to right or down.**

henw _ _ _ _        sah _ _ _

oubrhgt _ _ _ _ _ _ _

tou _ _ _        esog _ _ _ _

eadha _ _ _ _ _        yb _ _

eeshp _ _ _ _ _        fo _ _

eciov _ _ _ _ _        lla _ _ _

llsca _ _ _ _ _        ish _ _ _

mean _ _ _ _        eh _ _

deals _ _ _ _ _        wno _ _ _

wlloof _ _ _ _ _ _

mih _ _ _

useebca _ _ _ _ _ _ _

| H | O | W | N | B | H | I | S | F | X |
| I | X | S | H | E | E | P | H | O | B |
| M | V | O | I | C | E | A | A | L | R |
| L | X | B | C | A | L | L | S | L | O |
| E | X | Y | O | U | T | L | N | O | U |
| A | G | O | E | S | H | E | A | W | G |
| D | X | W | H | E | N | X | M | O | H |
| S | X | A | H | E | A | D | E | F | T |

**Across**

The Bible is special because it has the _____ of Jesus.

**Down**

We spend time with our good shepherd in _____.

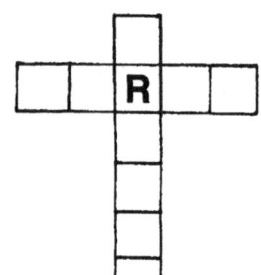

20

Lent 4

**The Good Shepherd is the gate.**

**The words that are underlined are in the word search puzzle. They will go down or left to right.**

When Jesus lived there were lots of sheep. Everyone knew about sheep and shepherds and how shepherds loved their sheep very much and would do everything possible to take good care of them. So when Jesus said he was the good shepherd, he hoped everyone who heard him would understand how, like a shepherd, he loves us and wants us to be a part of his flock and to take care of us. Shepherds took care of their sheep night and day. They would see that their sheep had plenty to eat and drink. At night they checked each one and put medicine on any hurts. The flock slept in a walled-in place and the shepherd lay down across the opening to sleep. The shepherd became the door, or gate, and could guard his sheep from wild animals or thieves. They were safe. Jesus said he was the shepherd. He is the door, or gate. We can only enter into his flock through believing and following Jesus. Jesus' sheep come in and go out and find pasture. That means life with Jesus is safe in his care. Let us ask him to be our shepherd!

| W | A | S | K | X | J | E | S | U | S | T |
|---|---|---|---|---|---|---|---|---|---|---|
| I | X | S | N | C | O | M | E | N | U | H |
| L | S | H | E | P | H | E | R | D | S | I |
| D | G | E | W | N | T | A | K | E | E | E |
| P | U | E | D | I | X | C | A | R | E | V |
| A | A | P | R | G | A | T | E | S | X | E |
| S | R | F | I | H | W | A | N | T | S | S |
| T | D | L | N | T | X | L | D | A | Y | G |
| U | O | O | K | X | G | O | X | N | S | O |
| R | O | C | I | L | O | V | E | D | A | O |
| E | R | K | N | Z | U | E | A | A | F | D |
| Z | X | H | U | R | T | S | T | T | E | Z |

**Did you know ...**
The shepherd carried a staff, sometimes called a crook. It was about five feet long with a curved end. Sheep sometimes got into dangerous places. With the curved end around the sheep's chest or back legs, the shepherd could catch it and pull it back to safety.

**Down**
Jesus is the gate we enter _____.

**Across**
Then we become part of his _____.

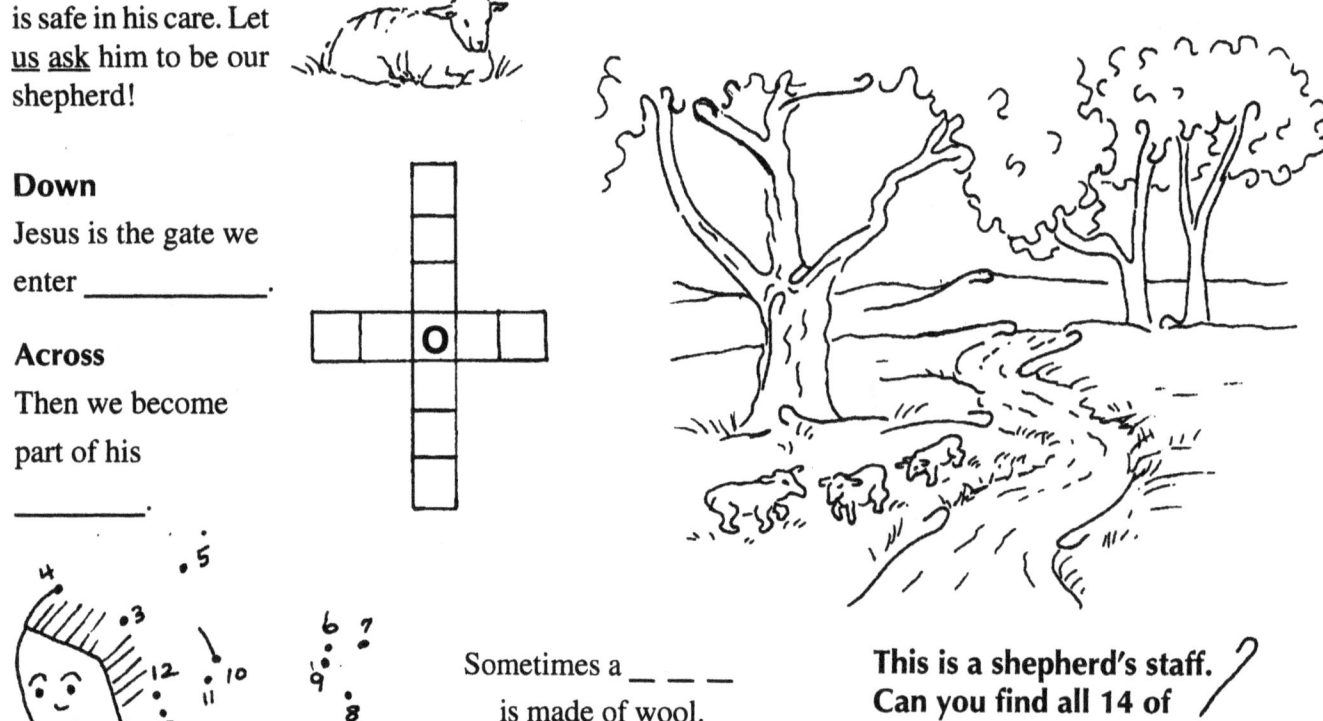

Sometimes a _ _ _ is made of wool.

This is a shepherd's staff. Can you find all 14 of them in the picture above?

Lent 5

**The Good Shepherd has other sheep.**

**Draw a line to the word that finishes each sentence correctly. Then find the same words in the word search puzzle below.**

| | |
|---|---|
| Jesus said he was the good | different |
| Shepherds love their | shepherd |
| When shepherds call the sheep, the sheep | places |
| Shepherds lived with their sheep day and | sheep |
| That's why they knew each other very | together |
| Jesus lived on | come |
| He taught us about God's | sisters |
| We can be sheep in Jesus' | night |
| We must believe in | me |
| With our ears we | well |
| We must listen to him and | Father |
| Jesus loves | you |
| Jesus loves | earth |
| Jesus said others are part of his flock | too |
| Jesus loves people who are | love |
| Jesus loves people who live other | follow |
| Loving Jesus brings people | hear |
| Loving Jesus makes God our | flock |
| Loving Jesus makes us brothers and | him |

**Down**
Jesus said that he was the good _____.

**Across**
He said that he had _____ sheep and that we would all be in one flock together.

Sometimes _ _ _ _ _ are made of wool.

```
F  L  O  C  K  D  Y  O  U
H  X  S  X  N  I  G  H  T
I  Z  H  Y  Z  F  M  E  O
M  W  E  L  L  F  T  O  O
S  H  E  P  H  E  R  D  X
I  X  P  X  Z  R  X  L  H
S  F  A  T  H  E  R  O  E
T  C  O  M  E  N  X  V  A
E  T  O  G  E  T  H  E  R
R  P  L  A  C  E  S  X  T
S  F  O  L  L  O  W  Z  H
```

**Did you know ...**
There are at least 200 kinds of sheep. Sheep are all sizes, large and small. Some of them have long wool and some short. Some have soft, fine wool while others have wool that is coarse. The best wool comes from young sheep. Millions of pounds of wool are produced every year in the United States, but Australia leads the world in wool production.

**Lent 6/Passion Sunday**

**The Good Shepherd will give his life for his sheep.**

**Did you know ...**
The shepherd carried a rod. This was a club about three feet long, usually made from oak with a bulging joint forming a knot on the end. Sometimes the big end had pieces of sharp flint or metal. The rod was a weapon used to beat away wolves. He also carried a sling. A shepherd was very good with a sling. He could toss a pebble in front of a wandering sheep to warn it to turn back. He could throw a stone about the size of his fist from his sling to kill or drive away dangerous animals. But wild animals were not the only danger. The shepherd also had to guard against thieves trying to steal. Some shepherds really did die trying to protect their sheep.

**Down**
Jesus is a _____ shepherd. He willingly died to save us.

**Across**
He died on a _____ to pay for our sins.

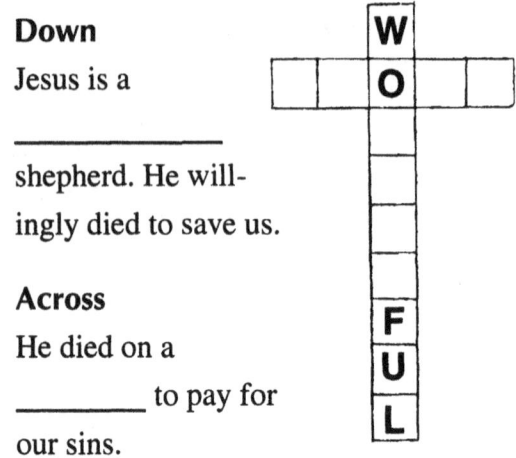

Do you know what the shepherd boy, David, did with a sling and a stone? You can read the story in 1 Samuel 17.

**Jesus said this:**
"I lay down my life for the sheep."
John 10:15b

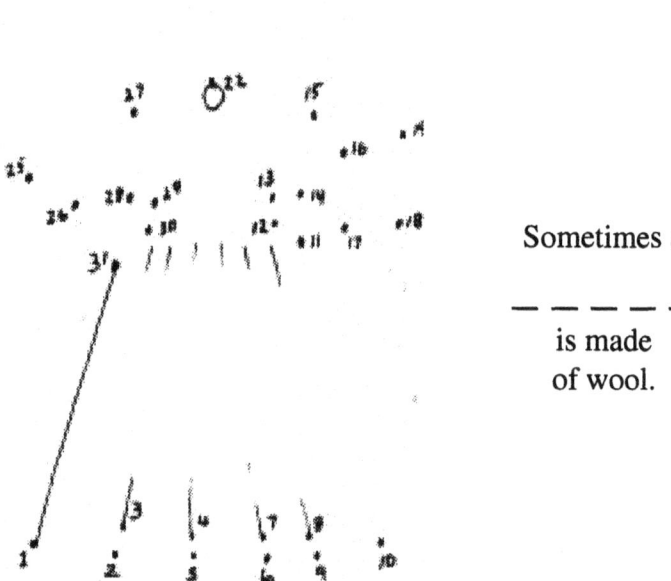

Sometimes a
_ _ _ _ _
is made of wool.

**Fill in the blanks to make complete words using the vowels a, e, i, o, or u. When you have completed them, find the same words in the word search puzzle.**

Jesus is our sh_‍ph_rd. He c_r_s for us like a g_ _d shepherd will care f_r his sheep. Where Jesus lived there were n_ f_nc__s. A sheep could get l_st. The shepherd would hunt until he f_ _nd a lost sheep. Then he would r_j_ _c_. There is rejoicing _n heaven too when s_m_ _n_ becomes p_rt of Jesus' fl_ck. The r_ _l shepherd loves his sheep and is willing t_ d_ _ to protect them from w_ld _n_m_ls or th_ _v_s. Jesus is like that. Jesus died for us. Jesus is a wonderful shepherd!

| F | X | P | A | R | T | C | Z |
|---|---|---|---|---|---|---|---|
| O | F | L | O | C | K | A | S |
| R | O | T | S | X | W | R | H |
| E | U | H | O | D | I | E | E |
| A | N | I | M | A | L | S | P |
| L | D | E | E | I | D | T | H |
| O | D | V | O | N | O | O | E |
| S | F | E | N | C | E | S | R |
| T | X | S | E | G | O | O | D |
| X | R | E | J | O | I | C | E |

**Easter Sunday**

**Jesus is our Good Shepherd.**

**Fill in the blanks using words from the list below.**

Good shepherds love their sheep and take good care of each one. They know all their sheep's _ _ _ _ _ and all about each one. They know if one is _ _ _ _ or nervous or likes to wander _ _ _ _. Shepherds and _ _ _ _ _ spend lots of _ _ _ _ together. The shepherd makes sure they have _ _ _ _ _ _ to _ _ _ and drink. He puts _ _ _ _ _ _ _ _ on any sores. At _ _ _ _ _ he sleeps across the entrance to the _ _ _ _ _ and guards them. He becomes the _ _ _ _. Nothing can _ _ _ _ his sheep. A good _ _ _ _ _ _ _ _ loves his sheep so much he is willing to die to _ _ _ _ _ _ _ them. Jesus said, "I _ _ the _ _ _ _ shepherd." He said, "My sheep hear my _ _ _ _ _ and they _ _ _ _ _ _ me." If we _ _ _ _ and believe in Jesus and _ _ what he says, we are his sheep. He said he was the gate. We must enter through Jesus to become part of his flock. Jesus said he has other sheep and we will all be _ _ _ flock. Jesus said he will lay down his life but _ _ will take it up again. Jesus is no ordinary shepherd. He is God's Son and he died for us, but he lives again and continues to be our shepherd.

| hurt | gate | he |
| shepherd | flock | am |
| protect | night | lazy |
| voice | medicine | names |
| follow | eat | |
| love | plenty | |
| one | time | |
| good | sheep | |
| do | away | |

**Use the list of words for the word search puzzle. They go left to right or down.**

| G | L | H | U | R | T | F | H | E | G |
| O | O | N | F | O | L | L | O | W | A |
| O | V | A | W | A | Y | O | T | O | T |
| D | E | M | E | D | I | C | I | N | E |
| P | L | E | N | T | Y | K | M | E | A |
| E | A | S | H | E | E | P | E | X | M |
| A | Z | S | H | E | P | H | E | R | D |
| T | Y | P | R | O | T | E | C | T | O |
| V | O | I | C | E | N | I | G | H | T |

"My sheep hear my voice. I know them, and they follow me. I give them eternal life, and they will never perish."
John 10:27-28

**Across**
_____ is alive!

**Down**
He continues to be our good _____ providing us with abundant life now and forever.

**Unscramble the words to find what Jesus said.**
I ma eht oodg ershephd. John 10:14

_ _ _ _ _ _ _ _ _ _ _ _ _ _ .

28

Easter 1

**Jesus asked Peter to feed his sheep.**

**Did you know ...**
There are still large flocks of sheep. In our country they are mostly in the western states. There are shepherds or sheepherders who spend many hours caring for the sheep. Often their only companions for days are their dog and horse. A dog is a great help rounding up stray sheep. It shares the shepherds' work, food, and camp. These shepherds often ride horseback to watch over their sheep. The flock has to be guarded from coyotes, cougars, and stray dogs. Sheep have to be moved often so they won't eat so much that they ruin a pasture. Spring is the very busy time when babies are born. Often the ewe, or mother, needs the shepherd's help, so shepherds work day and night caring for mothers and lambs. Sometimes a mother does not live, then the shepherd will have to bottle-feed the lamb. The flock is brought to corrals for sheepshearing after all the lambs are born in late spring. The wool is gathered into large bags and sent to market.

**If the sentence tells how to be a shepherd's helper, mark it with a T. If it does not, mark it with an F.**
___ I invite a friend to Sunday school.
___ I listen to the Sunday school teacher.
___ I do not like her.
___ I will not share my candy.
___ I will give some of my allowance.
___ I laugh at his mistakes.
___ I help her carry the books.
___ I help my brother with homework.
___ I smile a lot.
___ I tell Mom and Dad I love them.

**Across**
Jesus fills an

_____ place

in our life.

**Down**
We can be a

_____

helper when we share Jesus and his love with others.

**Use the list of words for the word search puzzle. They go left to right or down.**

| hungry | how | with | them |
| empty | share | joy | yes |
| unhappy | love | we | now |
| Jesus | to | can | me |
| fills | others | help | yes |
| life | feed | | |

| W | H | U | N | G | R | Y | X | Y |
| O | X | N | X | T | H | E | M | E |
| T | X | H | X | J | E | S | U | S |
| H | C | A | N | O | L | M | E | H |
| E | M | P | T | Y | P | X | Z | A |
| R | F | P | F | I | L | L | S | R |
| S | E | Y | T | W | I | T | H | E |
| X | E | Z | O | E | F | H | O | W |
| X | D | L | O | V | E | N | O | W |

Sometimes there is wool in the

_ _ _ on the floor.

# Answer Keys For Children's Activity Pages

# ANSWER KEYS

## Pages 16, 18, 20

The words that are underlined are in the word search puzzle. They will go down or left to right.

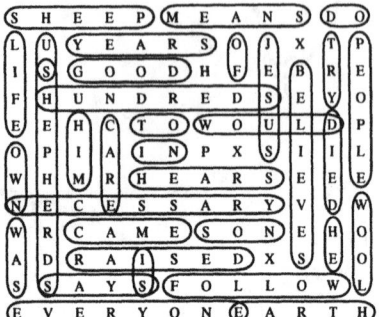

People have been using <u>wool</u> from <u>sheep</u> for <u>hundreds</u> of <u>years</u>. When <u>Jesus</u> lived, there were <u>shepherds</u> who took care <u>of</u> sheep. A good shepherd <u>would</u> do everything <u>necessary</u> to take good <u>care</u> of his sheep. Jesus said he <u>was</u> the <u>good</u> shepherd. <u>Everyone</u> who <u>believes</u> in him, <u>hears</u> him, and follows <u>him</u> are his sheep. <u>To</u> believe in Jesus means that we believe he <u>is</u> God's <u>own</u> <u>son</u> who <u>came</u> to <u>earth</u>, <u>died</u> for <u>us</u>, and was <u>raised</u> to <u>life</u> again. To <u>follow</u> Jesus <u>means</u> that we love him and we <u>try</u> hard to <u>do</u> what <u>he</u> <u>says</u>.

**Across**
<u>sheep</u> are animals that need lots of care.

**Down**
A <u>shepherd</u> is someone who gives that care.

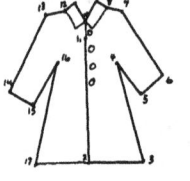

Sometimes a <u>c o a t</u> is made of wool.

**Can you unscramble these words? They are all found in the Bible verses below.**

ownk <u>k n o w</u>     peesh <u>s h e e p</u>
mhte <u>t h e m</u>     em <u>m e</u>
icevo <u>v o i c e</u>   wno <u>o w n</u>
odog <u>g o o d</u>     ololwf <u>f o l l o w</u>
rhae <u>h e a r</u>     erdshpeh <u>s h e p h e r d</u>

**Jesus said this:**
"I am the good shepherd. I know my own and my own know me."    John 10:14

"My sheep hear my voice. I know them and they follow me."    John 10:27

**Did you know ...**
A shepherd dressed for comfort and convenience. He wore an undergarment called a tunic. Over this he wore a four-foot square wool cloak which shielded him from sun, rain, or snow. He could pull it over his head like a tent for shelter at night. It usually had big grey and black stripes and was woven by his wife or daughters. He folded a piece of cloth around his waist and kept small things in that. It was called a girdle. The shepherd had a veil for his head. It was about 36-inches square and was folded into a triangle and kept in place by a ring of twisted goat's hair. He had long hair and a beard because that was easiest to care for.

---

The words that are underlined are in the word search puzzle. See if you can find them.

There is <u>something</u> that is all ours and <u>very</u> <u>special</u> to us. It is our <u>name</u>. It is <u>sometimes</u> <u>hard</u> to <u>remember</u> everyone's name. But <u>Jesus</u> knows <u>all</u> of <u>our</u> names. He <u>knows</u> all <u>about</u> us, too, just like a <u>shepherd</u> knew the name of each <u>sheep</u> <u>in</u> his flock. He knew all about <u>each</u> <u>one</u> <u>too</u>, because shepherds who <u>kept</u> sheep for their <u>wool</u> <u>lived</u> with their sheep many <u>years</u>, taking <u>care</u> of them. Jesus is the <u>good</u> shepherd. He <u>loves</u> each one of <u>us</u>. <u>If</u> we <u>listen</u> to <u>him</u> and follow him, <u>we</u> are sheep of his <u>flock</u>.

**Did you know ...**
Sheep were raised for many purposes. They provided food, meat, milk, and fat from the tail. Sheep horns could be made into a musical instrument or a flask, which is a bottle. Sheep were used as sacrifices in worship. They provided clothing; sometimes the whole skin was used, but more often the wool was cut, spun, and woven into clothing for all the family. Cutting sheep wool was done in late spring and was a time of celebration, for the wool was valuable. Friends were often invited to share a happy meal during this time of celebration.

Sometimes a <u>b l a n k e t</u> is made of wool.

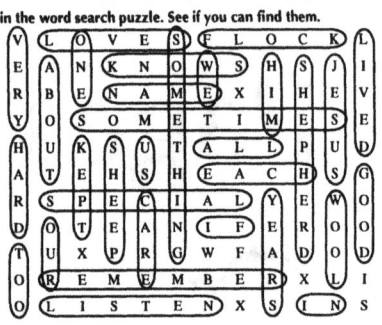

**Down**
Jesus, the good shepherd, <u>knows</u> our name.

**Across**
Jesus knows all <u>about</u> us.

**Use the words below to finish the sentences.**
Sheep were <u>valuable</u>.
They were kept for their <u>wool</u>.
Shepherds loved their <u>sheep</u>.
They knew the names of <u>all</u>.
Sheep come when the shepherd <u>calls</u>.
Our name is <u>special</u>.
Name tags help us <u>remember</u>.
Jesus is the good <u>shepherd</u>.
He knows our <u>name</u>.
He knows all about <u>us</u>.
He loves us just like we <u>are</u>.
We need to follow <u>him</u>.
We will do as he <u>says</u>.

are
says
shepherd
remember
special
valuable
wool
sheep
all
name
us
him
calls

---

This sheep wants to spend time with the shepherd. Help it find the way.

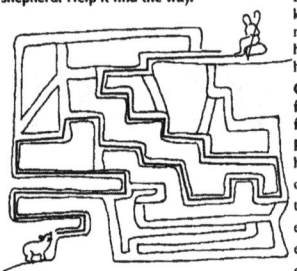

**Jesus said this:**
I am the good shepherd. I know my own and my own know me. He [the shepherd] calls his own sheep by name and leads them out. When he has brought out all his own, he goes ahead of them and the sheep follow him because they know his voice.   (John 10:14, 3, 5)

**Can you unscramble these words? They are all found in the Bible verses above. When you are finished, find the same words in the word search puzzle. They will go left to right or down.**

henw <u>w h e n</u>     sah <u>h a s</u>
oubrhgt <u>b r o u g h t</u>
tou <u>o u t</u>     esog <u>g o e s</u>
eadha <u>a h e a d</u>     yb <u>b y</u>
eeshp <u>s h e e p</u>     fo <u>o f</u>
eciov <u>v o i c e</u>     lla <u>a l l</u>
llsca <u>c a l l s</u>     ish <u>h i s</u>
mean <u>n a m e</u>     eh <u>h e</u>
deals <u>l e a d s</u>     wno <u>o w n</u>
wlloof <u>f o l l o w</u>
mih <u>h i m</u>
useebca <u>b e c a u s e</u>

**Did you know ...**
If all the sheep were doing well and the shepherd had a little free time, he would sometimes make a musical pipe from reeds, which were a kind of grass with a hollow stem. Sometimes he used a ram's horn to play music. A ram is a male sheep.

The Bible tells us that before David became king of Israel, he was a shepherd. He played a lyre, sometimes called a harp. He played so well that he was asked to play for the king. This story is found in 1 Samuel 16:12-23.

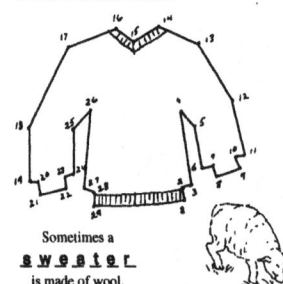

Sometimes a <u>s w e a t e r</u> is made of wool.

**Across**
The Bible is special because it has the <u>words</u> of Jesus.

**Down**
We spend time with our good shepherd in <u>prayer</u>.

32

# ANSWER KEYS

## Pages 22, 24, 26

**The words that are underlined are in the word search puzzle. They will go down or left to right.**

When Jesus lived there were lots of sheep. Everyone <u>knew</u> about <u>sheep</u> and shepherds and how <u>shepherds</u> <u>loved</u> their sheep very much and would do everything possible to <u>take</u> good <u>care</u> of them. So when Jesus said he was the <u>good</u> shepherd, he hoped everyone who heard him would understand how, like a shepherd, he <u>loves</u> us and <u>wants</u> us to be a part of his flock and to take care of us. Shepherds took care of their sheep <u>night</u> and <u>day</u>. They would <u>see</u> that their sheep had plenty to <u>eat</u> and <u>drink</u>. At night they checked each one and put medicine on any <u>hurts</u>. The <u>flock</u> slept in a walled-in place and the shepherd lay down across the opening to sleep. The shepherd became the <u>door</u>, or gate, and could <u>guard</u> his sheep from <u>wild</u> animals or <u>thieves</u>. They were <u>safe</u>. Jesus said he was the shepherd. He is the door, or <u>gate</u>. We can only enter into his flock through believing and following Jesus. Jesus' sheep <u>come in</u> and <u>go out</u> and find <u>pasture</u>. That means life with Jesus is safe in his care. Let <u>us</u> <u>ask</u> him to be our shepherd!

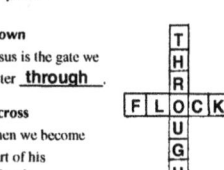

**Did you know ...**
The shepherd carried a staff, sometimes called a crook. It was about five feet long with a curved end. Sheep sometimes got into dangerous places. With the curved end around the sheep's chest or back legs, the shepherd could catch it and pull it back to safety.

**Down**
Jesus is the gate we enter **through**.

**Across**
Then we become part of his **flock**.

Sometimes a **h a t** is made of wool.

This is a shepherd's staff. Can you find all 14 of them in the picture above?

---

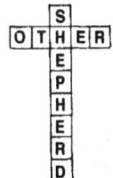

Draw a line to the word that finishes each sentence correctly. Then find the same words in the word search puzzle below.

Jesus said he was the good — shepherd
Shepherds love their — sheep
When shepherds call the sheep, the sheep — come
Shepherds lived with their sheep day and — night
That's why they knew each other very — well
Jesus lived on — earth
He taught us about God's — Father
We can be sheep in Jesus' — flock
We must believe in — him
With our ears we — hear
We must listen to him and — follow
Jesus loves — you
Jesus loves — me
Jesus said others are part of his flock — too
Jesus loves people who are — different
Jesus loves people who live other — places
Loving Jesus brings people — together
Loving Jesus makes God our — Father
Loving Jesus makes us brothers and — sisters

**Down**
Jesus said that he was the **shepherd**

**Across**
He said that he had **other** sheep and that we would all be in one flock together.

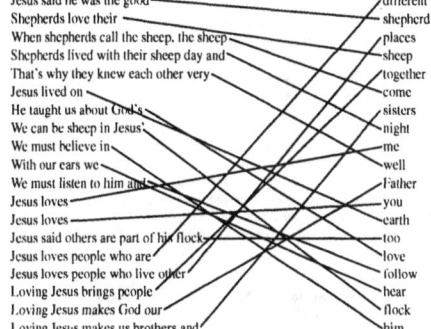

Sometimes **p a n t s** are made of wool.

**Did you know ...**
There are at least 200 kinds of sheep. Sheep are all sizes, large and small. Some of them have long wool and some short. Some have soft, fine wool while others have wool that is coarse. The best wool comes from young sheep. Millions of pounds of wool are produced every year in the United States, but Australia leads the world in wool production.

---

**Did you know ...**
The shepherd carried a rod. This was a club about three feet long, usually made from oak with a bulging joint forming a knot on the end. Sometimes the big end had pieces of sharp flint or metal. The rod was a weapon used to beat away wolves. He also carried a sling. A shepherd was very good with a sling. He could toss a pebble in front of a wandering sheep to warn it to turn back. He could throw a stone about the size of his fist from his sling to kill or drive away dangerous animals. But wild animals were not the only danger. The shepherd also had to guard against thieves trying to steal. Some shepherds really did die trying to protect their sheep.

Do you know what the shepherd boy, David, did with a sling and a stone? You can read the story in 1 Samuel 17.

**Jesus said this:**
"I lay down my life for the sheep."
John 10:15b

**Fill in the blanks to make complete words using the vowels a, e, i, o, or u. When you have completed them, find the same words in the word search puzzle.**

Jesus is our sh**e**ph**e**rd. He c**a**r**e**s for us like a g**o** **o**d shepherd will care f**o**r his sheep. Where Jesus lived there were n**o** f**e**nc**e**s. A sheep could get l**o**st. The shepherd would hunt until he f**o** **u**nd a lost sheep. Then he would r**e**j**o** **i** c**e**. There is rejoicing **i**n heaven too when s**o**m**e o**n**e** becomes p**a**rt of Jesus' fl**o**ck. The r**e** **a**l shepherd loves his sheep and is willing t**o** d**i** **e** to protect them from w**i**ld **a**n**i**m**a**ls or th**i** **e**v**e**s. Jesus is like that. Jesus died for us. Jesus is a wonderful shepherd!

**Down**
Jesus is a **wonderful** shepherd. He willingly died to save us.

**Across**
He died on a **cross** to pay for our sins.

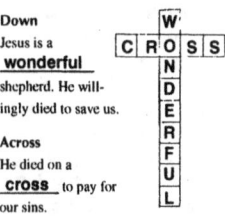

Sometimes a **d r e s s** is made of wool.

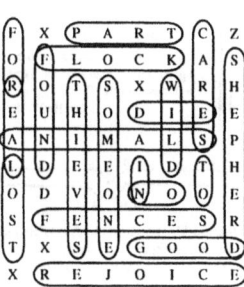

# ANSWER KEYS

## Pages 28, 30

**Fill in the blanks using words from the list below.**
Good shepherds love their sheep and take good care of each one. They know all their sheep's **n a m e s** and all about each one. They know if one is **l a z y** or nervous or likes to wander **a w a y**. Shepherds and **s h e e p** spend lots of **t i m e** together. The shepherd makes sure they have **p l e n t y** to **e a t** and drink. He puts **m e d i c i n e** on any sores. At **n i g h t** he sleeps across the entrance to the **f l o c k** and guards them. He becomes the **g a t e**. Nothing can **h u r t** his sheep. A good **s h e p h e r d** loves his sheep so much he is willing to die to **p r o t e c t** them. Jesus said, "I **a m** the **g o o d** shepherd." He said, "My sheep hear my **v o i c e** and they **f o l l o w** me." If we **l o v e** and believe in Jesus and **d o** what he says, we are his sheep. He said he was the gate. We must enter through Jesus to become part of his flock. Jesus said he has other sheep and we will all be **o n e** flock. Jesus said he will lay down his life but **h e** will take it up again. Jesus is no ordinary shepherd. He is God's Son and he died for us, but he lives again and continues to be our shepherd.

hurt — gate — he
shepherd — flock — am
protect — night — lazy
voice — medicine — names
follow — eat
love — plenty
one — time
good — sheep
do — away

**Use the list of words for the word search puzzle. They go left to right or down.**

G (L) (H U R T) F (H E) G
O O (F O L L O W) A
O V (A W A Y) O T T
D E (M E D I C I N E)
(P L E N T Y) K M E A
E A (S H E E P) E X M
A Z (S H E P H E R D)
T (P R O T E C T) O
(V O I C E) (N I G H T)

"My sheep hear my voice. I know them, and they follow me. I give them eternal life, and they will never perish."
John 10:27-28

**Unscramble the words to find what Jesus said.**
I ma eht oodg ershephd. John 10:14
**I am the good shepherd**

**Did you know ...**
There are still large flocks of sheep. In our country they are mostly in the western states. There are shepherds or sheepherders who spend many hours caring for the sheep. Often their only companions for days are their dog and horse. A dog is a great help rounding up stray sheep. It shares the shepherds' work, food, and camp. These shepherds often ride horseback to watch over their sheep. The flock has to be guarded from coyotes, cougars, and stray dogs. Sheep have to be moved often so they won't eat so much that they ruin a pasture. Spring is the very busy time when babies are born. Often the ewe, or mother, needs the shepherd's help, so shepherds work day and night caring for mothers and lambs. Sometimes a mother does not live, then the shepherd will have to bottle-feed the lamb. The flock is brought to corrals for sheepshearing after all the lambs are born in late spring. The wool is gathered into large bags and sent to market.

**If the sentence tells how to be a shepherd's helper, mark it with a T. If it does not, mark it with an F.**
T  I invite a friend to Sunday school.
T  I listen to the Sunday school teacher.
F  I do not like her.
F  I will not share my candy.
T  I will give some of my allowance.
F  I laugh at his mistakes.
T  I help her carry the books.
T  I help my brother with homework.
T  I smile a lot.
T  I tell Mom and Dad I love them.

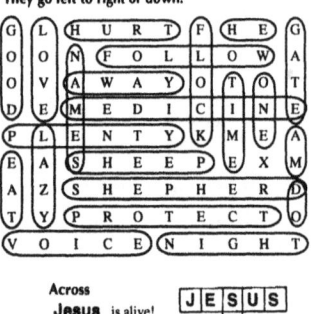

**Across**
**Jesus** is alive!
**Down**
He continues to be our good **shepherd** providing us with abundant life now and forever.

J E S U S
  H
  E
  P
  H
  E
  R
  D

**Across**
Jesus fills an **empty** place in our life.
**Down**
We can be a **shepherd's** helper when we share Jesus and his love with others.

S
H
(E M P T Y)
P
H
E
R
D
S

**Use the list of words for the word search puzzle. They go left to right or down.**

hungry — how — with — them
empty — share — joy — yes
unhappy — love — we — now
Jesus — to — can — me
fills — others — help — yes
life — feed

W (H U N G R Y) X Y
O X N X (T H E) M E
T X H X (J E S U S)
H (C A N) O L (M E) H
(E M P T Y) P X Z A
R (F P (F I L L S) R
S E E (T) (W I T H)
X E Z O (F) (H O W)
X (D) (L O V E) (N O W)

Sometimes there is wool in the **r u g** on the floor.

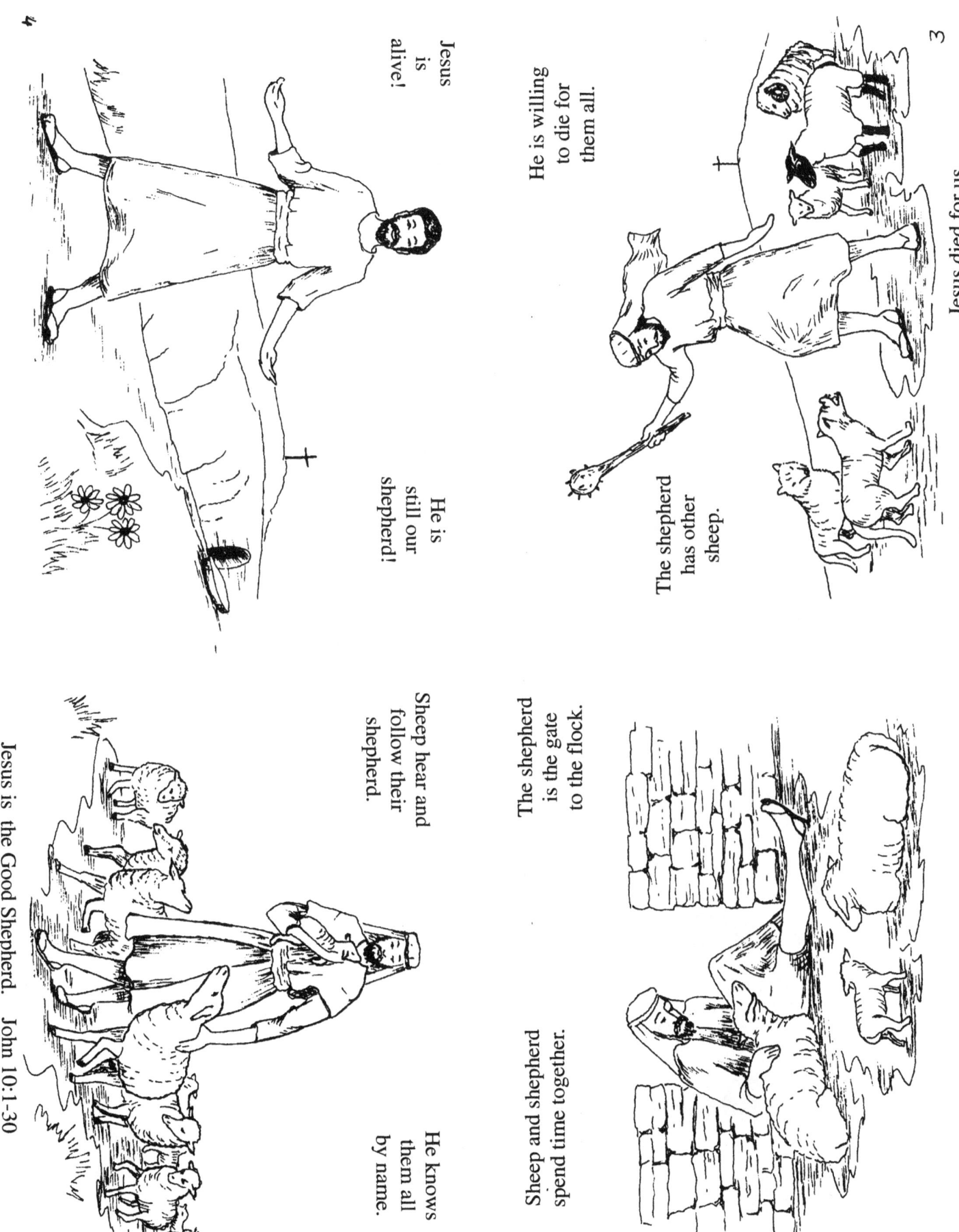

Jesus is the Good Shepherd. John 10:1-30

Sheep hear and follow their shepherd.

He knows them all by name.

Sheep and shepherd spend time together.

The shepherd is the gate to the flock.

The shepherd has other sheep.

He is willing to die for them all.

Jesus died for us.

Jesus is alive!

He is still our shepherd!

www.ingramcontent.com/pod-product-compliance
Lightning Source LLC
Chambersburg PA
CBHW081503040426
42446CB00016B/3373